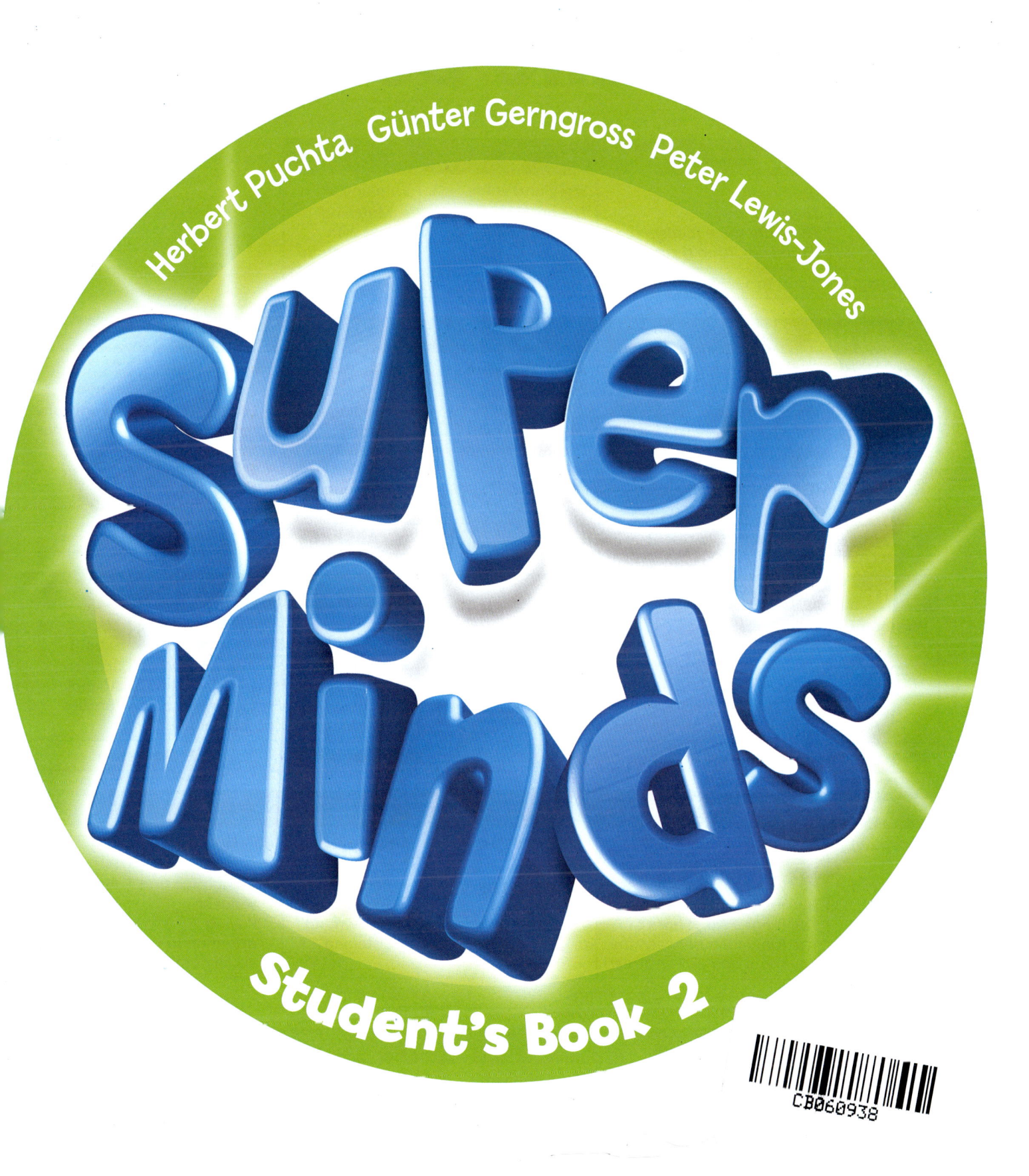

Herbert Puchta Günter Gerngross Peter Lewis-Jones

Super Minds

Student's Book 2

CB060938

CAMBRIDGE
UNIVERSITY PRESS

Map of the book

Back to school (pages 4–9)

Vocabulary	Grammar	Story and value	Thinking skills
The classroom	There's a (car). There are some (balls). (Stand up). (Don't) stand up.	The burglars Helping people	Matching text with information

🚩 **Song:** It's good to see you all again

1 My day (pages 10–21)

Vocabulary	Grammar	Story and value Phonics	Skills	Thinking skills	English for school
Daily routines	What's the time? It's (nine) o'clock. When do you (have lunch)? At (one) o'clock. (Claire gets up) at (eight) o'clock.	What a day! Offering to help The letter sounds ee and ea	• Reading and writing • Listening and speaking	• Logical-mathematical thinking • Selecting and classifying	**Geography:** Time zones

🚩 **Song:** It's three o'clock in the afternoon   🚩 Creativity   🚩 Revision

2 The zoo (pages 22–33)

Vocabulary	Grammar	Story and value Phonics	Skills	Thinking skills	English for school
Animals	(Freddy) likes / doesn't like (spiders). Does (Mark/Emma) like (bananas)? Yes, he/she does.	The zoo keeper Helping people The letter sounds ie and y	• Reading, listening and writing • Speaking	• Applying world knowledge • Classifying and categorising	**Science:** Animal families

🚩 **Song:** The zebra likes sausages   🚩 Creativity   🚩 Revision

3 Where we live (pages 34–45)

Vocabulary	Grammar	Story and value Phonics	Skills	Thinking skills	English for school
Places in a town	Has your town got a (swimming pool)? Yes, it has. / No, it hasn't. The (cinema) is between the (toy shop) and (Green Street).	The tree on the track Perseverance The letter sounds tr, gr and dr	• Reading, speaking and writing • Listening	• Comparing and sequencing • Paying attention to visual details	**Art:** Towns and art

🚩 **Song:** Our town's got a lot of great things   🚩 Creativity   🚩 Revision

4 The market (pages 46–57)

Vocabulary	Grammar	Story and value Phonics	Skills	Thinking skills	English for school
Food	Would you like a (tomato) / some (bread)? Are there any (pears)? Yes, there are. Is there any (bread)? No, there isn't any.	Bad apples Cheating doesn't pay The letter sounds w and wh	• Reading, speaking and writing • Listening	• Matching visual and written information • Applying world knowledge and interpreting	**Science:** Bacteria and food

🚩 **Song:** Would you like some fruit?   🚩 Creativity   🚩 Revision

5 My bedroom (pages 58–69)

Vocabulary	Grammar	Story and value Phonics	Skills	Thinking skills	English for school
Furniture	I like this/that (book). I like these/those (book)s. Whose (sock)s are these? They're (Fred)'s. Whose (hat) is this? It's (May)'s.	Tidy up! Tidiness The letter sound oo	• Reading • Listening, speaking and writing	• Reflecting and analysing • Analysing	Science: Recycling

▶ Song: Little Timothy McKane   ▶ Creativity   ▶ Revision

6 People (pages 70–81)

Vocabulary	Grammar	Story and value Phonics	Skills	Thinking skills	English for school
The face	Are you (angry)? No, I'm (tired). / Yes, I'm (angry). Our/Their birthdays are in (May).	Thunder's birthday Being a good loser The letter sounds a_e, ai and ay	• Reading and writing • Listening and speaking	• Interpreting and giving reasons • Sequencing and remembering	Science: The life cycle of a butterfly

▶ Song: Who's that man over there?   ▶ Creativity   ▶ Revision

7 Off we go! (pages 82–93)

Vocabulary	Grammar	Story and value Phonics	Skills	Thinking skills	English for school
Transport	I'd like to go to (Africa) by (plane). What are you doing? I'm (fly)ing (a plane).	The bus trip Being generous The letter sounds u_e, ew, ue and oe	• Speaking • Listening, reading and writing	• Matching • Predicting and checking	Maths: Measuring

▶ Song: It's a big, wide world out there   ▶ Creativity   ▶ Revision

8 Sports club (pages 94–105)

Vocabulary	Grammar	Story and value Phonics	Skills	Thinking skills	English for school
Sport	(Flying a kite)'s difficult. What sport do you like doing? I like (swimming). So do I. / I don't.	The football club Including people The letter sounds o, oa and o_e	• Listening, speaking and writing • Reading	• Comparing and evaluating • Evaluating and selecting	Science: Breathing

▶ Song: Playing tennis is great fun   ▶ Creativity   ▶ Revision

9 Holiday plans (pages 106–117)

Vocabulary	Grammar	Story and value Phonics	Skills	Thinking skills	English for school
Holidays	Can I/we (go horse riding) (tomorrow morning)?	Dream holidays Helping people The letter sounds z and s	• Reading • Listening and speaking	• Matching text with visual information	Literature: Fairy tales

▶ Song: It's time for a holiday   ▶ Creativity   ▶ Revision

● **Festivals and cut-outs:** pages 118–128   ● **Stickers:** End section

Grammar 3

Back to school

1 🎧 CD1 02 **Listen and look. Then listen and say the words.**

1) door
2) bookcase
3) wall
4) clock
5) window
6) board
7) cupboard
8) chair
9) floor

2 🎧 CD1 03 **Listen and chant.**

Touch the window,
Touch the door,
Touch the cupboard,
Touch the floor.

Touch the bookcase,
Touch the wall,
Touch the board,
And that is all!

The classroom

1 Listen, look and number the sentences.

☐ There are some books.   ☐ There's an apple.

☐ There's a clock.   ☐ There are some rulers.

2 Grammar focus — Listen and say.

There's a car.   **There are some** balls.

3 Play the action game.

There are some kites …

There's / There are

5

1 🎵 **Listen and sing.**

It's good to see you all again.
Welcome back!
Enjoy your English class again.
Welcome back!

10, 20, 30, snap,
40, 50, 60, tap,
70, 80, 90, slap,
It's good to see you all again.

11, 22, 33, snap,
44, 55, 66, tap,
77, 88, 99, slap,
And now 100, clap, clap, clap!

It's good to see you all again …

★BINGO★

30	11	55
44	66	20
99	80	100

2 Choose nine numbers from the song. Make a bingo card and play the game.

Singing for pleasure; numbers 10 to 100

1 🎧 CD1 09 **Think!** Listen and number the pictures. Then read and draw lines.

a Sit down.

b Open your book.

c Don't sit down.

d Don't stand up.

e Don't open your book.

f Stand up.

2 🎧 CD1 10 **Grammar focus** Listen and say.

Stand up.   **Don't** stand up.
Sit down.   **Don't** sit down.

3 Play the listening game.

Stand up.

Imperatives 7

1 The burglars

1) Bye! — Now let's go home.

2) Whisper, there's a problem at your school. — Let's go to the school. Quick! — Now?

3) Can you check this out, Flash? — No problem.

4) There are two burglars taking our computer. — What can we do? — I've got an idea. Wait here!

5) Ooooooh! — What's that?

6) Aaargghh! — There are some monsters in here. — Let's go!

Value: helping people

7
- Don't drop the computer!
- OK.
- The burglars!

8
- Close the door!
- OK!

9
- We've got them!

10
- Well done.
- Great work.
- Yes!

2 Read and tick (✓) the boxes.

1. There are three burglars at the school.   yes ☐ / no ☐
2. The burglars are taking a computer.   yes ☐ / no ☐
3. The burglars have got two cars.   yes ☐ / no ☐
4. The burglars drop the computer.   yes ☐ / no ☐
5. The children stop the burglars.   yes ☐ / no ☐

1 My day

1 🎧 CD1 13 Listen and look. Then listen and say the words.

1. get up
2. get dressed 
3. have breakfast 
4. brush your teeth 
5. go to school 
6. have lunch 
7. play in the park 
8. have dinner 
9. go to bed 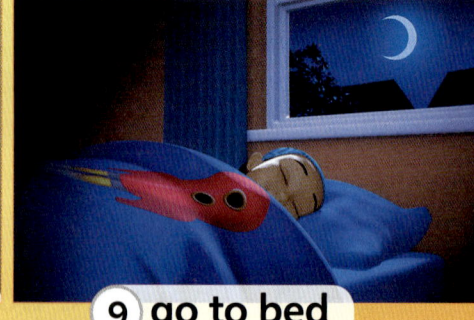

2 🎧 CD1 14 Listen and chant.

Get up early,
Yawn, yawn, yawn.
Have your breakfast,
Crunch, crunch, crunch.
Brush your teeth,
Brush, brush, brush.

Go to school,
Run, run, run.
Have some lunch,
Munch, munch, munch.
Go out and play,
Hip, hip, hurray!

Daily routines

1 Listen and colour.

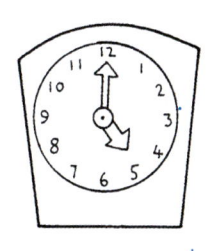

2 Listen and draw the times on the clocks.

3 Grammar focus — Listen and say.

What's the time? It's nine o'clock.
When do you have breakfast? At seven o'clock.

4 Ask and answer.

When do you … ?

At … o'clock.

Telling the time

1 **Listen and sing.**

It's three o'clock in the afternoon!

I get dressed,
And then I have a shower.
And then I brush my teeth,
For another hour.

Mr, Mr, Mr Blue,
What a funny thing to do.
Oh, Mr, Mr Blue,
What can we do with you?

It's six o'clock in the morning!

I eat dinner,
And watch TV.
Then I have lunch,
And drink some tea.

Mr, Mr, Mr Blue,
What a funny thing to do.
Oh, Mr, Mr Blue,
What can we do with you? ...

2 **Draw a picture of Mr Blue.**

I play the piano in the bath.

Singing for pleasure

1 Read and number the pictures.

Benny gets up at seven o'clock. He has breakfast at eight o'clock and then he goes to school. He plays in the park at four o'clock. He has dinner with his mum and dad at six o'clock and he goes to bed at nine o'clock.

2 Grammar focus — Listen and say.

Claire **gets up at** eight **o'clock**.
She **goes to school at** nine **o'clock**.

3 Think! Look and say what the children do.

Present simple, 3rd person

1 What a day!

1. Oh no!

2. Not again.

3. Careful, Thunder. — Oops!

4. What's the problem, Mum? — Can you see my keys? They're under the car.

5. Careful, Thunder! — Sorry, Mum!

6. Mmm! I love chicken. It's not such a bad day after all.

Value: offering to help your parents

7 Bedtime. Hurray!

8 No!

2 **What does Thunder do at these times?**   Thunder … at seven o'clock.
   1 seven o'clock   2 four o'clock   3 six o'clock
   4 three o'clock   5 eight o'clock

3 **Find who says …**   Can you see my keys?

4 **Listen and say.**

Eat your cheese and peas! Then brush your teeth, please.

Phonics focus 15

Skills

1 **Read and circle.**

Janice is a pilot. She flies from Heathrow airport in London to all over Europe. At eleven o'clock in the morning she leaves her house. She arrives at the airport at twelve o'clock. Today, her flight is to Rome. It leaves London at three o'clock and it arrives in Italy at five o'clock. At seven o'clock, the plane leaves Rome and it arrives in London at ten o'clock. Janice gets home at eleven o'clock at night. What a long day for Janice!

1 Janice leaves her house.

2 Janice arrives at the airport.

3 Her plane leaves London.

4 Her plane arrives in Rome.

5 Her plane leaves Rome.

6 Janice gets home.

2 **Choose a day of the week, draw pictures and write about it.**

On Saturday I get up at nine o'clock and have breakfast at ten o'clock.

Skills

1 🎧 CD1 28 Listen and draw lines.

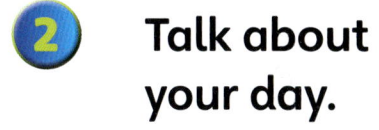

2 Talk about your day.

"I get up at … I have breakfast at …"

Listening and speaking

TIME ZONES

1 **Listen, read and look at the map.**

In the world there are lots of different time zones. When it is twelve o'clock in London, in summer, it is seven o'clock in the evening in Beijing, but it is only six o'clock in the morning in Mexico City. What time is it in New York and Cairo?

2 **Think!** **Read and complete.**

1 When it is one o'clock in the afternoon in London, it is _____ o'clock in the morning in New York.

2 When it is eleven o'clock in the morning in London, it is _____ o'clock in the afternoon in Cairo.

3 When it is two o'clock in the afternoon in London, it is _____ o'clock in the evening in Beijing.

4 When it is four o'clock in the afternoon in London, it is _____ o'clock in the morning in Mexico City.

Geography

Learn and think

1 **Project** Make a clock.

2 Play games with your clock.

In New York it's three o'clock in the afternoon. What's the time in Mexico City?

It's two o'clock in the afternoon.

Geography 19

Do that!

1 🎧 CD1 30 Listen and act out with your teacher.
Then listen again and number the pictures.

2 Read and number the sentences from the story.

☐ Oh no! There's milk all over you.   ☐ Get dressed.
☐ Clean your jumper.   ☐ Get your schoolbag.
☐ Run into the bathroom.   ☐ Have breakfast.
☐ Stop. Where's your schoolbag?   ☐ Run to school.

3 Listen to your friend and act out.

Run to school.

20 Creativity

1 **Think!** Make a poster.

My time to do things

a Draw a big table on a big piece of paper.

b Write *morning*, *afternoon*, *evening* and the times on the left-hand side.

c On pieces of paper, write things you do and draw pictures. Stick your pieces of paper on the table at the times you do them.

2 Talk about when you do things.

> I have lunch at one o'clock in the afternoon.

Revision 21

2 The zoo

1 🎧 CD1 31 Listen and look. Then listen and say the words.

1. zebra
2. monkey
3. hippo
4. parrot
5. snake
6. bear
7. tiger
8. crocodile

2 🎧 CD1 32 Listen and chant.

Come on, let's go to the zoo!
Come on, let's go to the zoo!
Hippo, zebra, monkey, bear,
Parrot, tiger, all are there.
Come on, let's go to the zoo!
It's fun for me and you.

22 Animals

1 Look, read and write the names.

1 Monica the monkey likes bananas.
2 Mary the monkey doesn't like cheese.
3 Tony the tiger likes chicken.
4 Tim the tiger doesn't like carrots.
5 Ben the bear likes apples.
6 Bill the bear doesn't like peas.

2 CD 1 33 **Grammar focus** Listen and say.

Freddy **likes** spiders.   Freddy **doesn't like** apples.

3 Draw an animal. Tell your friends about it.

This is Freddy the frog. He lives in a tree and he eats spiders. He doesn't like apples.

Likes / Doesn't like 23

1 **Listen and sing.**

The zebra likes sausages,
He doesn't like peas.
Some carrots and sausages,
For the zebra, please.

Peas, peas, lovely peas.
Someone come and eat them,
My lovely peas.

The hippo likes bananas,
She doesn't like peas.
Some apples and bananas,
For the hippo, please.

Peas,
peas ...

The parrot likes sandwiches,
He doesn't like peas.
Some pizza and sandwiches,
For the parrot, please.

Peas, peas ...

2 **Ask and answer.**

What does the zebra like?   The zebra likes ...

Singing for pleasure

1 Read and draw lines.

1 Does the baby mouse sleep a lot?
2 Does it eat fruit?
3 Does it play?
4 Does it like swimming?

a No, it doesn't like swimming.
b Yes, it does. It sleeps all day.
c No, it doesn't. It drinks milk.
d Yes, it does. It plays with its mother.

2 Grammar focus — Listen and say.

Does Mark **like** bananas?   Yes, he **does**.
Does Emma **like** bananas?   No, she **doesn't**.

3 Look at the table. Ask and answer.

	bananas	apples	cheese	fish
Mark	☺	☹	☹	☺
Emma	☹	☺	☺	☺

Questions and answers with *Does ... like?*

The zoo keeper

1. Look at the monkey.

2. The zoo keeper doesn't know what to do. Help! Let's help him.

3. Got you! Wow!

4. How does he do that?

5. Come here, snake. Yes, Whisper.

6. No, my keys! Don't throw them. I can help.

26 Value: helping people

7 Great, Misty!

8 Here you are.

Thank you all so much!

2 Match the Super Friends with the animals.

Whisper catches the …

3 Find who says … My keys!

4 Listen and say.

Mike flies by pies in the sky.

Phonics focus 27

Skills

1 Read and tick (✓) the boxes.

Hipsway Zoo
Open 10:00 – 6:00

Come and see our animals. What's your favourite animal? Is it the lion? The elephant? The hippo? What about the crocodiles, or the snakes? We have 100 different kinds of animals. Our big bird house is famous. Come inside and see beautiful birds flying over your head. Is there something you want to know about an animal? Our zoo keepers can answer all your questions. When you're hungry, you can visit the café for lunch. We've got lots of delicious food and drink.

1. There are crocodiles at the zoo.   yes ☐ / no ☐
2. You can talk to the zoo keepers.   yes ☐ / no ☐
3. There are two cafés at the zoo.   yes ☐ / no ☐
4. The zoo opens at six o'clock.   yes ☐ / no ☐

2 CD 1 · 42 Listen and answer.

1. What's the parrot called?
2. Where's she from?
3. How old is she?
4. What's her favourite food?

1. The parrot is called …

3 Write about an animal. Can your friends guess what it is?

My favourite animal is very small. It likes cheese but it doesn't like cats. What is it?

Reading, listening and writing

Skills

1 Sticker — Listen to your teacher and stick.

2 Look and say. "The cheese is …"

Speaking 29

Learn and think

Animal families

1 🎵 CD1 44 **Listen and read about animal family groups.**

Every animal is part of a family group. The animals in each family group have features that make them different from other animal family groups. Here are some examples of features.

eggs 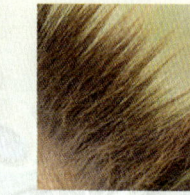   hair    feathers    scales    blood

2 **Think!** **Look at some groups and write the missing features.**

can often fly   their babies drink milk   have six legs   lay eggs

Mammals
- have hair
- have warm blood
-

mouse    bear

Reptiles
- have scales
- have cold blood
-

crocodile    lizard

Birds
- lay eggs
- have feathers
-

owl     duck

Insects
- lay eggs
- have cold blood
-

butterfly    beetle

30 Science

Learn and think

1 **Think!** Look and stick in the animal family groups.

Does it lay eggs?   Can it fly?   Does it have babies?

mammals   birds

reptiles   insects

2 **Project** Make an animal family group display.

Science 31

Create that!

1 🎧 CD 1, 45 **Listen and imagine. Then draw your picture.**

2 **Show your picture to your friends.**

> This is my animal. It's half bear and half mouse. It climbs trees. It's small and brown. It likes cheese and honey.

> This is my animal. It's half lion and half crocodile. It's very beautiful. It's yellow and green. It likes parrots for breakfast and frogs for lunch.

Act out at the zoo

1 **Look, read and plan.**

Is there something you want to know about an animal?
Our zoo keepers can answer all your questions.

HIPPO FACTSHEET

- the hippo comes from Africa
- it lives in rivers
- it eats grass
- it's very dangerous

Useful language

Child	Zoo keeper
Where does the … come from?	It comes from …
Is it dangerous?	Yes, it is. / No, it isn't.
What does it eat?	It eats …
Can it … ?	Yes, it can. / No, it can't.
Thank you.	You're welcome.

2 **Act out your play.**

Where does the hippo come from?

It comes from Africa.

Revision

3 Where we live

1 🎧 CD2 02 **Listen and look. Then listen and say the words.**

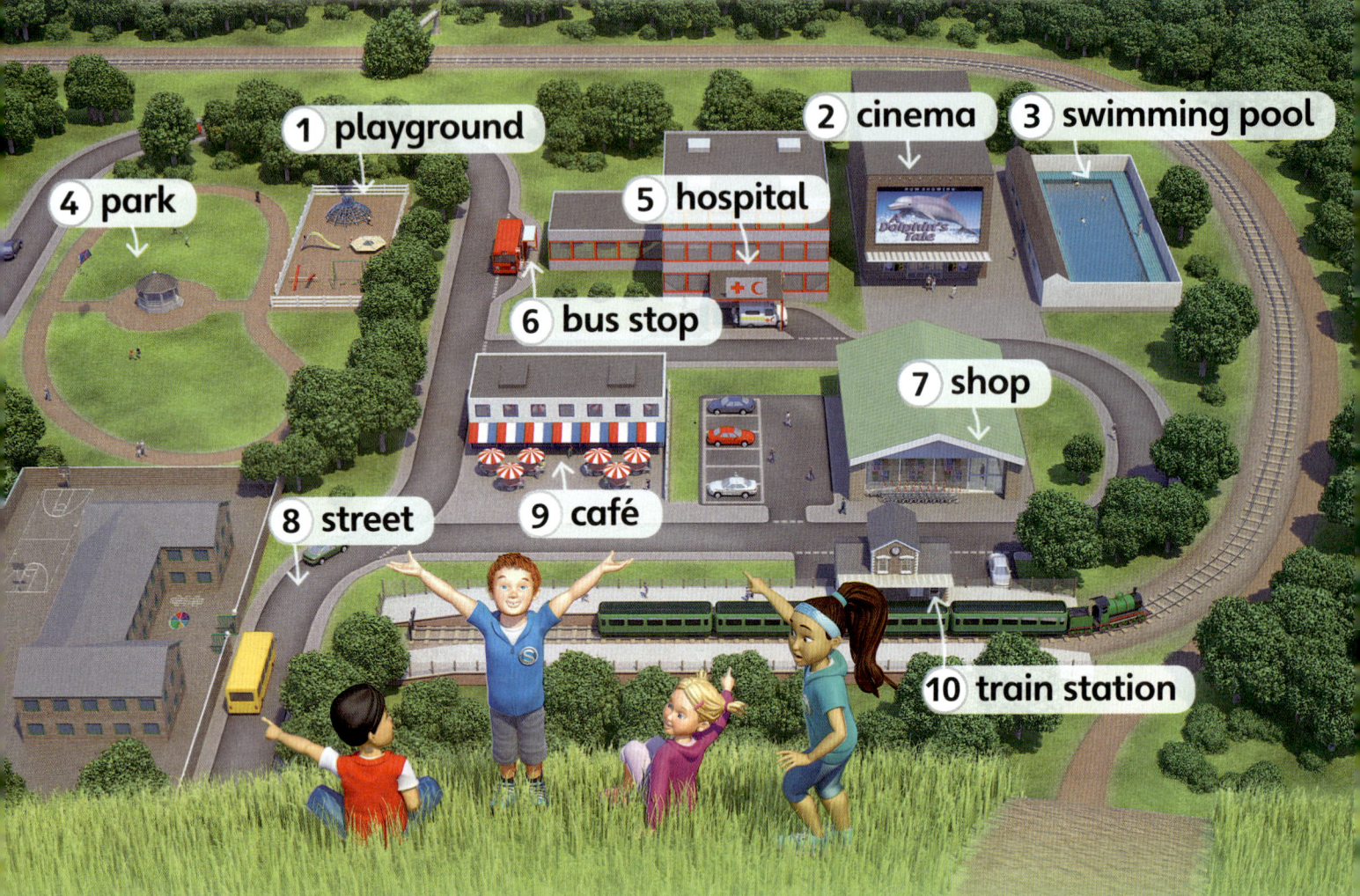

1. playground
2. cinema
3. swimming pool
4. park
5. hospital
6. bus stop
7. shop
8. street
9. café
10. train station

2 🎧 CD2 03 **Listen and chant.**

Can you see the shop?
Yes, we can.
Can you see the bus stop?
Yes, we can.

Shop, street, park and pool.
Looking from up here,
Is really cool.

Can you see the school?
Yes, we can.
Can you see the pool?
Yes, we can.

Shop, street, park and pool.
Looking from up here,
Is really cool.

34 Places in a town

1 Look at the picture. Read and circle.

1 Has Top Town got a cinema?   Yes, it has. / No, it hasn't.

2 Has Top Town got a café?   Yes, it has. / No, it hasn't.

2 **Grammar focus** Listen and say.

Has your town **got** a swimming pool? Yes, it **has**.
Has your town **got** a train station?   No, it **hasn't**.

3 Imagine a town and write five things it has got. Then ask and answer.

Has your town got … ?

No, it hasn't. It's got …

1 **Listen and sing.**

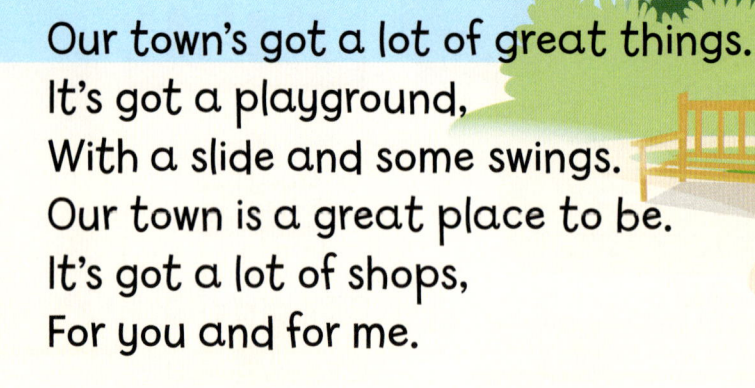

Our town's got a lot of great things.
It's got a playground,
With a slide and some swings.
Our town is a great place to be.
It's got a lot of shops,
For you and for me.

Our town! Come to our town.
Our town! Come on, everyone.
Our town! Come to our town.
Our town! Come and have some fun ...

Our town is a great place to stay.
It's got a park,
Where we can play all day.
Our town's got a nice swimming pool.
Jump into the water,
It's nice and cool.

Our town! Come to our town ...

2 **Think!** Listen again and number the pictures.

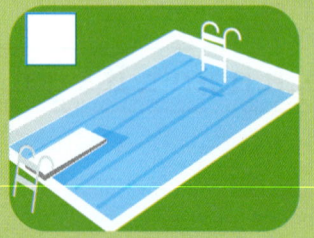

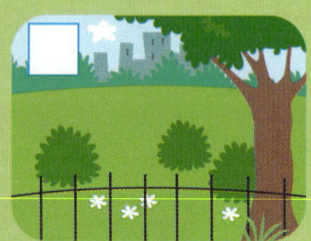

Singing for pleasure

1 **Listen and write the words.**

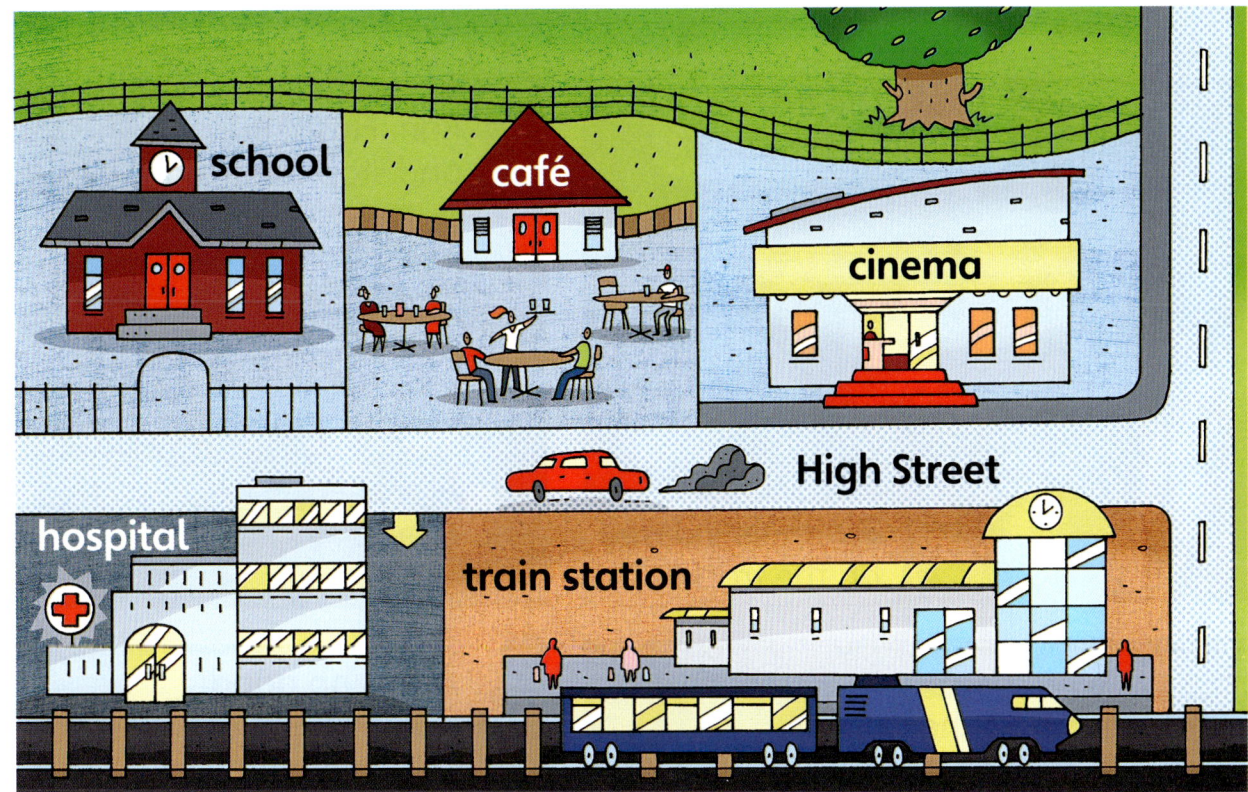

1. The café is between the school and the _____.
2. The car is in front of the _____.
3. The hospital is next to the _____.
4. The tree is behind the _____.

2 **Grammar focus** **Listen and say.**

The cinema is **between** the toy shop and Green Street.
The hospital is **behind** the playground.

3 **Decide where to put these places on your map.**

toy shop   zoo   sweet shop   car   tree

Now tell your partner about your map.

Prepositions

1 The tree on the track

1
Look. The train is leaving the station.
But there's a tree on the track!

2
Run, Flash! Run and stop the train!
OK.

3
Stop! Stop the train!
Wow. She's fast!

4
It's no good. Hmm. Let's try something else.

5
She's next to my train again. What does she want?

6
S–T–O–P.

38 Value: perseverance

7

Stop!

8

Thanks, kids!

No problem.

2 Point to pictures in the story and make sentences.

The Super Friends are	on	the hill.
The driver is		the train.
	in	
The tree is		the track.
	next to	
Flash is		the station.
	in front of	
The train is		the town.

3 Find who says … But there's a **tr**ee on the **tr**ack!

4 CD2 12 Listen and say.

Troy's **gr**andpa's got a **gr**eat big **gr**een **dr**agon.

Phonics focus 39

Skills

1 Read and write the names.

Isabelle

Martin

My favourite place in town is the cinema. On Saturday mornings there is a Kids' Club. They show films for children. There are three different films. My mum and dad take me every week. Sometimes we have popcorn or sweets. _____

My favourite place in town is the café. My mum takes me and my brother there on Wednesdays. We go after school for our dinner. I have pizza and chips. My brother has chicken and rice. Then we have some cake. Delicious! _____

2 Read again and answer.

1. How many films does the cinema show at Kids' Club?
2. What does Martin eat at the cinema?
3. Who does Isabelle go to the café with?
4. What does Isabelle eat at the café?

3 Write about your favourite place.

My favourite place is London. I go there to see my grandmother. She lives by the river. We have lots of fun there.

4 Now tell your friends. (My favourite place is …)

Reading, speaking and writing

Skills

1 🎧 CD2 15 **Listen and tick (✓) the box. Where are they?**

1
- a) book shop
- b) café
- c) school

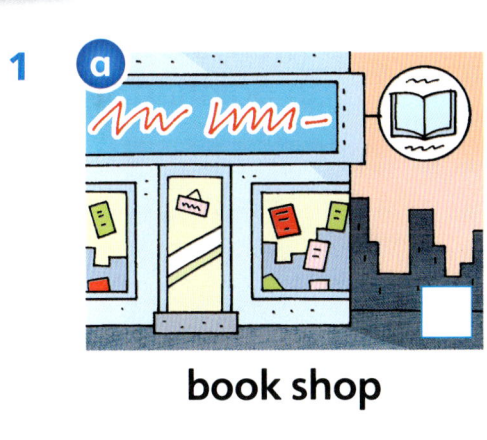

2
- a) swimming pool
- b) playground
- c) farm

3
- a) train station
- b) hospital
- c) cinema

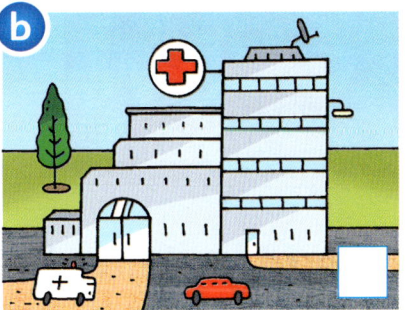

4
- a) farm
- b) zoo
- c) bus stop

Listening 41

Learn and think: Towns and art

1 Look and say. What is in the paintings?

> There's a lake in painting 1.

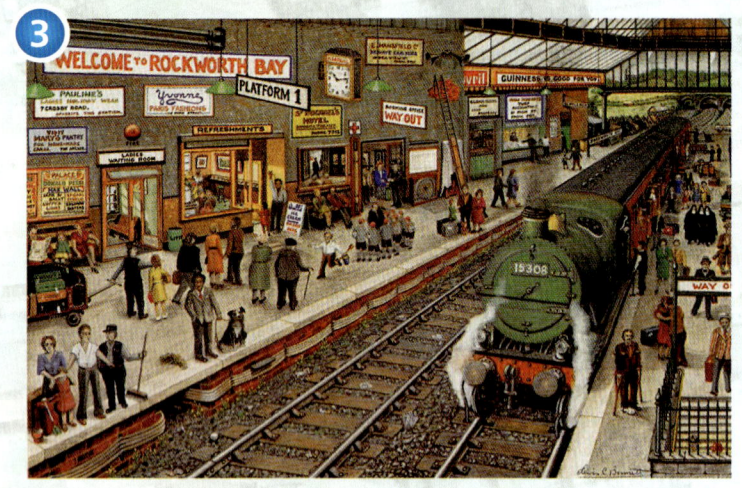

2 **Think!** Listen, read and number. Which painting are they talking about?

- I like the water and the big buildings. It's beautiful.
- I like the colours. Yellow, purple and green. I'd like to play there.
- I like this painting because I like trains.
- There are lots of stars in the sky. I like them.

3 Which painting is your favourite?

> I like … because …

42 Art

Learn and think

3

1 Where are these paintings?

> Painting 1 is in a playground.

① ② ③ ④

2 Where can you find paintings in your town?

> There is a painting in the playground.

> There are paintings in the café.

3 **Project** Make pictures of your town and create a collage.

Art 43

Do that!

1 🎧 CD2 17 **Listen and act out with your teacher. Then listen again and number the pictures.**

2 **Read and number the sentences from the story.**

☐ Go to the café. Buy some orange juice.

☐ Where's your train? It's gone!

☐ Run to the platform.

☐ Buy a magazine and read it.

☐ Buy a ticket.

☐ Drink your juice.

☐ Look at your watch. Oh no!

☐ Walk up the steps to the station.

3 **Listen to your friend and act out.**

Drink your juice.

44 Creativity

Quiz time

1 Where are they?
   a at the swimming pool   b at the bus stop
   c at the train station

2 Top Town hasn't got a …
   a   b   c

3 The boy … an ice cream.
   a have got   b has got   c hasn't got

4 Where is the cat?
   a between the dogs   b in front of the dogs
   c behind the dogs

5 Who stops the train?
   a   b   c

6 Circle the different sound.
   a **gr**ey   b **u**gly   c **gr**eat

7 Martin really likes the …
   a   b   c

8 What colour is the train in the painting on page 42?
   a green   b red   c blue

Revision 45

4 The market

1 Listen and look. Then listen and say the words.

1. grapes
2. beans
3. bread
4. lemons
5. tomatoes
6. fish
7. eggs
8. mangos
9. watermelons
10. potatoes

2 Listen and chant.

Apples, apples,
I am hungry,
Lemons, mangos,
Watermelons.
I am hungry,
Have some fruit!

Apples, apples,
I am thirsty,
Lemons, mangos,
Watermelons.
I am thirsty,
Have some juice!

1 Read and number the pictures.

1. Would you like an apple?
   Yes, please.
2. Would you like a tomato?
   No, thank you.
3. Would you like some bread?
   Yes, please.
4. Would you like an egg?
   No, thank you.

2 CD2 20 **Grammar focus** Listen and say.

Would you like a tomato? — Yes, please.
Would you like some bread? — No, thank you.

3 Tick (✓) four things you would like to eat. Then ask and answer.

Would you like ... ?   47

1 **Listen and sing.**

Would you like some fruit?
Yeah, fruit is really great.
Please eat lots of fruit,
Put it on your plate!
Would you like some fruit? ...

Give me a mango, please!
Give me an apple, too.
Give me some grapes,
And please keep some for you.

Would you like some fruit?
Yeah, fruit is really great.
Please eat lots of fruit,
Put it on your plate!
Would you like some fruit? ...

2 **Listen again and tick (✓) the fruit that you hear in the song.**

48 Singing for pleasure

1 **Listen and write the words.**

1 Are there any _____ ?
2 Are there any _____ ?
3 Is there any _____ ?
4 There isn't any _____ .
5 Is there any _____ ?
6 There aren't any _____ .

2 **Grammar focus** **Listen and say.**

Are there any pears in the fridge?	Yes, there **are**. No, there **aren't any**.
Is there any bread in the basket?	Yes, there **is**. No, there **isn't any**.

3 Choose where to stick your food. Then ask and answer.

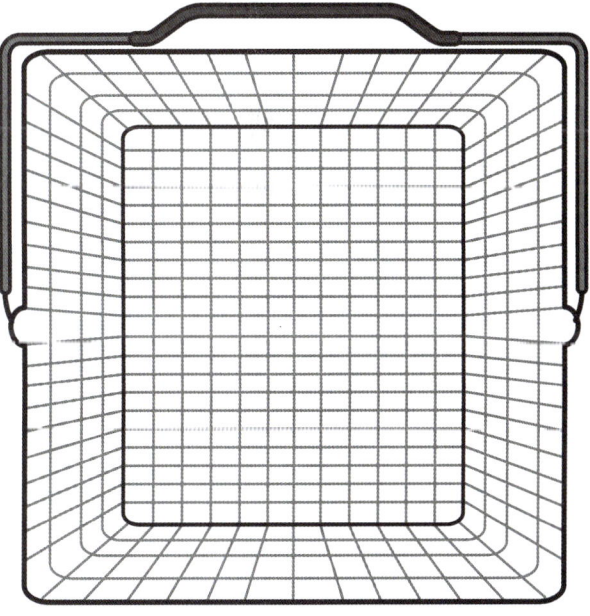

Are there / Is there any ... ? 49

1 Bad apples

1. Here are two apples for everyone.

2. Look! I've got a bad apple. — Me too! — So have I!

3. What can we do? — I've got an idea. Come to the market with me.

4. Apples. Nice, sweet apples!

5. The man has got a box with good apples and a box with bad apples. — We know what we can do!

6. Eight apples, please. — Here you are.

50 Value: cheating doesn't pay

7 Look, everybody!
Four bad apples!

8 A box of good apples and a box of bad apples.
Well done, children!

2 Think! Look at the picture and circle the correct sentence.

1 Look everybody!
2 Two for everyone.
3 Well done!
4 Come to the market with me.

3 Find who says … What can we do?

4 🎧 CD2 28 Listen and say.

Where's the **w**atermelon, **W**ally?

Phonics focus

Skills

1 **Think!** What's needed for the cake? Read and tick (✓) the boxes.

Make some banana cake.
1. Put a cup of milk in a bowl.
2. Mix two bananas with the milk in the bowl.
3. Put a cup of sugar and two cups of flour into the bowl.
4. Then put four big spoons of butter and two eggs into the bowl. Start mixing. Then put the mixture in a cake tin.
5. Bake the cake in the oven for one hour. Enjoy it with your friends!

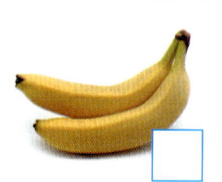

2 Act out the play.

Boy: Let's make some fruit juice for the party.
Girl: OK. Let's look in the fridge.
Boy: Are there any apples?
Girl: No, there aren't.
Boy: Are there any pears?
Girl: No, no pears.
Boy: What about oranges? Are there any oranges?
Girl: No, no oranges. No mangos, no pineapples.
Boy: What! No fruit at all?
Girl: Well, there are some grapes.
Boy: Grapes. Great! How many grapes are there?
Girl: Two.
Boy: OK. Let's just take a bottle of cola.

3 Write your own play and act it out.

Reading, speaking and writing

Skills

1 🎧 CD2 32 **Listen and tick (✓) the boxes.**

1 Who makes breakfast on Sunday?

a ☐   b ☐   c ☐

2 Who drinks milk for breakfast?

a ☐   b ☐   c ☐

3 Who eats eggs and beans for breakfast?

a ☐   b ☐   c ☐

4 Who doesn't like fruit?

a ☐   b ☐   c ☐

Listening 53

Learn and think: Bacteria and food

1 🎧 CD2 33 **Listen, read and number the photos.**

Bacteria are not animals, but they *are* living things. You can't see them because they are very, very small. There are lots of different bacteria. They have strange names! Here are some bacteria.

☐ **Listeria monocytogenes**  ☐ **E. coli** 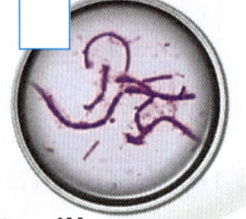 ☐ **Bacillus cereus** 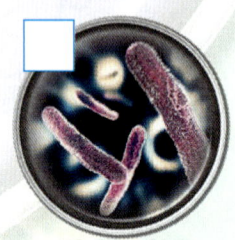 ☐ **Shigella**

2 🎧 CD2 34 **Listen, read and draw lines.**

Some bacteria are very dangerous. These bacteria can live in food and make us ill. We don't want to eat these bacteria. We need to be careful with food.

a

1 Clean the kitchen.

d

2 Keep different foods in different places before cooking.

b

e

3 Cook meat so it's very hot.

4 Wash fruit and vegetables.

c

5 Wash and dry your hands before you cook.

f

6 Keep food cold in the fridge.

54 Science

Learn and think

1 **Project** **Think!** Grow some bacteria.

1 Take half a lemon, put it on the ground.

2 Now put it in a clear plastic bag with a piece of wet tissue.

3 Leave the bag in a warm, dark place.

4 After a few days, take the bag out. Look at your lemon. Never eat food with this on!

Create that!

1 🎧 CD2 35 Listen and imagine. Then draw your picture.

2 Write about your picture. Then listen to your friends and guess.

In my favourite fruit salad, there are some oranges and there are some bananas. There aren't any grapes and there aren't any mangos. Yummy!

The food game

4

Revision 57

5 My bedroom

1 Listen and look. Then listen and say the words.

1. lamp
2. mirror
3. armchair
4. wardrobe
5. sofa
6. bed
7. table
8. mat

2 Listen and chant.

What a mess!
What a mess!
What a mess!
Please tidy up your room.

There's a schoolbag on the floor,
The jeans are on the armchair.
The T-shirt's on the lamp,
There's a plane under the bed.

There are pencils on the mat,
There's a ball on the table.
There's a book on the wardrobe,
And a sock on the clock.

Your cap's on the mirror,
Your train's on the sofa.
And where's the other sock?
On the chair, over there!

58 Furniture

1 **Listen and match.**

a Do you like these yellow chairs?

b I like this blue lamp.

c I don't like it. I like that green lamp over there.

d Yes, I do. And those blue chairs are nice too.

2 **Grammar focus** **Listen and say.**

I like **this** book.
I like **these** books.
I like **that** book.
I like **those** books.

3 **Talk about your classroom.**

I like those ...

I don't. I like the ...

This, that, these, those

1 **Listen and sing.**

Little Timothy McKane
Is a real pain.
His mum is in a shop with him.
Please stop it, stop it, Tim!

Do you like this sofa, Tim?
No, I don't. It's awful, Mum,
But that sofa over there,
Is beautiful, I swear!

Do you like these armchairs, Tim?
No, I don't. They're awful, Mum,
But those armchairs over there,
Are beautiful, beautiful, I swear!

Do you like this table, Tim?
No, I don't. It's awful, Mum,
But that table over there,
Is beautiful, I swear!

Do you like this sofa, Tim? ...

Little Timothy McKane ...

2 **Choose words and read out your verse.**

> Do you like these mirrors, Tim?
> No, I don't. They're awful, Mum,
> But those mirrors over there ...

60 Singing for pleasure

5

1 🎧 CD2 42 **Listen, read and tick (✓) the boxes.**

1 Whose jeans are these?
   They're ☐ Rosie's ☐ Nick's.

2 Whose cap is this?
   It's ☐ Bob's ☐ Mike's.

2 🎧 CD2 43 **Grammar focus** **Listen and say.**

| Whose socks are these? | They're Fred's. |
| Whose hat is this? | It's May's. |

3 **Look at the pictures. Then ask and answer.**

Whose ... this / these ... ? **61**

1 Tidy up!

1 Hello, it's Whisper. Can Flash come to the park?

Sorry, Whisper, not now. She's tidying up her room.

2 I don't like tidying up. Ah, I've got an idea!

3 First the clothes – jeans, sweaters, caps, shoes and socks!

4 Now the school things and the toys! Bag, books, balls and dolls. Ha!

5 Finished! Can I go to the park now?

Just a minute. Let me check first.

6 Wow! The room is really tidy now.

Value: tidiness

7 "Oh, your T-shirt. Let's put it in the wardrobe."

"No, Mum, no!"

8 "I don't believe it!"

"Sorry, Mum. No park for me today."

2 Imagine you are Whisper and Flash. Act out the phone call at the end of the story.

"Hi, Flash. It's Whisper again. Can you come to the park now? …"

"Hi, Whisper. Sorry, there's a problem …"

3 Find who says …

"Bag, books, balls and dolls."

4 Listen and say.

L**oo**k at the b**oo**ks all over the r**oo**m!

Phonics focus

Skills

1 Read and write the correct words next to numbers 1–8.

table   books   chairs   bed   clock   mirror   bookcase   wardrobe

My room

In my room there's a big, blue (1)_____ . There is a brown (2)_____ and there is a (3)_____ . On it there is my computer. There is a (4)_____ on the wall. There are also two (5)_____ in my room, but there isn't a (6)_____ . There is also a red (7)_____ . I think there are fifteen (8)_____ in it.

Skills

1 🎧 **Listen and answer.**

1. Where does Claire go when she wants to think?
2. Where does she sit?
3. What does she do?
4. Where do *you* go when you want to think?
5. What do you do?

1. Claire goes …

2 **What do you do when you want to think? Tell your friend.**

> When I want to think, I go to my room. I listen to music. I like music.

Listening, speaking and writing

Recycling

Learn and think

1 🎧 CD 2 50 **Think!** **Listen, read and talk about the question.**

We throw things away every day. This is called rubbish. A lot of rubbish goes into big holes in the ground called landfills. Landfills are bad for our world. This is why recycling is a good idea. What things do we throw away?

2 🎧 CD 2 51 **Listen and read about recycling. Number the pictures.**

When we recycle, we take rubbish and make it into new things.

1 We can make old newspapers and magazines into new paper.
2 We can make old bottles and jars into new glass.
3 We can make metal from fridges into new metal.
4 We can make old fruit and vegetables into earth for the garden.

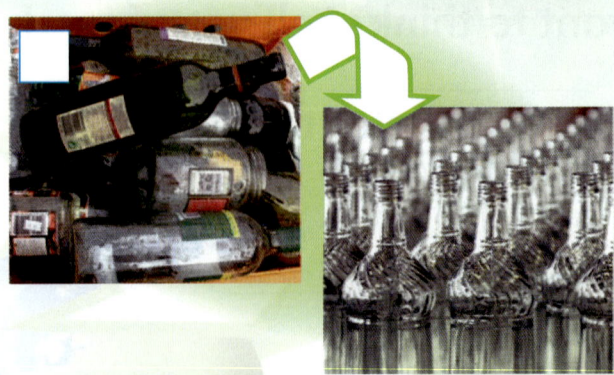

Science

Learn and think

1 Look, read and stick the rubbish in the correct bins.

FRUIT & VEGETABLES

GLASS

PAPER & CARD

METAL

2 Think! Think of more things to put in these bins.

We can put magazines in the paper bin.

3 Project Make some recycling bins for your classroom.

When you throw something away, think about which bin you put it in.

Science 67

Do that!

1 🎵 CD 2 · 52 **Listen and act out with your teacher.
Then listen again and number the pictures.**

2 **Read and number the sentences from the story.**

- Look in the wardrobe.
- Oh no!
- Where's your hat?
- Look out of the window.
- Look under your bed.
- The cat has got it.
- It's cold outside.
- Nothing!

3 **Listen to your friend and act out.**

Nothing!

68 Creativity

Quiz time

1 What's on the wall?
  a a picture and a clock
  b a mirror and a clock
  c a mirror and a picture

2 Do you like … orange clock over there?
  a this   b that   c those

3 Tim thinks this sofa is …
  a beautiful.   b old.   c awful.

4 What's in the room?
  a a bed and a desk
  b a desk and a wardrobe
  c a wardrobe and a bed

5 … cap is this?
  a Who   b What   c Whose

6 What does Flash leave on the lamp?
  a a T-shirt   b socks   c trousers

7 Circle the different sound.
  a b**oo**k   b d**o**ll   c l**oo**k

8 Rubbish is … for the environment.
  a not good   b not bad   c very good

Revision 69

6 People

1 Listen and look. Then listen and say the words.

1. eyes
2. hair
3. ears
4. glasses
5. nose
6. cheeks
7. mouth
8. chin
9. face

2 Listen and chant.

Her hair is brown,
It's brown, so brown.
Her nose is small,
It's small, so small.
Her eyes are blue,
They're blue, so blue.
Do you know her name?
I do. It's Sue.

His face is pink,
It's pink, so pink.
His eyes are green,
They're green, so green.
His hair is black,
It's black, so black.
Do you know his name?
Oh, yes. It's Jack.

The face

1 Read and write the names.

a　b　c　d　e　f

_____ _____ _____ _____ _____ _____

1. Tom has got green eyes and brown hair. He is sad.
2. Jim has got blue eyes and black hair. He is excited.
3. Sue has got blue eyes and she is wearing glasses. She is scared.
4. Dan has got brown eyes and brown hair. He is tired.
5. Sally has got brown hair and green eyes. She is wearing glasses. She is angry.
6. Paula has got blue eyes and brown hair. She is happy.

2 **Grammar focus** Listen and say.

Are you angry?　No, I'm not angry. I'm tired.
Are you happy?　Yes, I'm happy and I'm excited.

3 Play the mime game.

Are you … ?

Am / Is / Are + adjective

1 **Listen and sing.**

Who's that man over there,
The man with white hair?
The man with the guitar,
Who sings like a star …

That man is my grandpa,
The best one in the world.
He knows so many songs,
I love to sing with him …

Who's that woman over there,
The woman with grey hair?
The woman with grey hair,
In the rocking chair …

That woman is my grandma,
She's happy and she's great.
And I'm her best friend,
Although I'm only eight …

2 **Draw a picture of someone in your family and write about them.**

That boy is my brother.
He's friendly and he's fun …

1 Listen and chant.

The months are easy to remember:

January, February, March,
April, May and June,
July, August, September,
October, November, December.
Remember? No?
Then start again: January, February ...

2 Listen, read and circle.

1 Ben's birthday is in June / May.

2 Lucy's birthday is in May / April.

3 Tim and Sam's birthdays are in May / July.

Happy Birthday Lucy

3 Grammar focus — Listen and say.

Our birthdays are in May.
Their birthdays are in November.

4 Find out when your friends' birthdays are. Then play the birthday game.

Our birthdays are in …

Their birthdays are in …

The months; *our, their*

1 Thunder's birthday

1. Pull, pull, pull, you can win this tug of war!

2. Oh no! We're the winners.

3. Let's have a three-legged race. Great. I want to be with Flash, please.

4. Help! Oh dear. No medal for us.

5. Let's play *Pin the tail on the donkey*. Great!

6. That's perfect, Misty. Misty's great!

74 Value: being a good loser

7 "You aren't wearing your blindfold! That's not fair!"

8 "No medals for us today."
"Bye!"

2 Think! **Look at the picture and circle the correct sentence.**

1 That's not fair!
2 We're the winners!
3 Let's have a race.
4 Let's play.

3 Find who says … "Let's play *Pin the tail on the donkey*."

4 Listen and say.

Jane and a sn**a**ke m**a**ke c**a**kes on a r**ai**ny d**ay**.

Phonics focus 75

Skills

1 Think! Read, think and write what's missing in each birthday invitation.

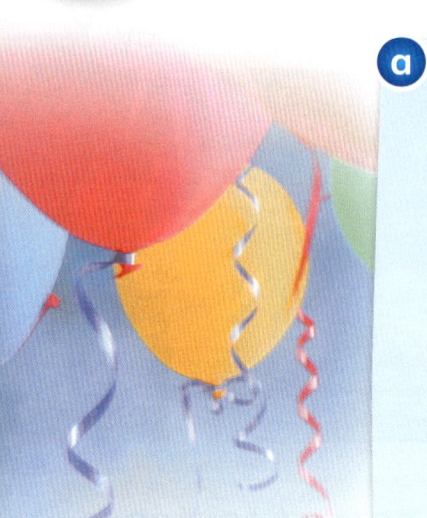

a

Dear Ben,
Come to my birthday party on Sunday. Please ask your sister to come, too. Can you also bring your football? I can't find mine. The birthday party is in our garden. See you on Sunday,
Tim

b

Dear Oliver,
Please come to my birthday party on Saturday. Can you bring your running shoes? We'll have a race. Mum says don't bring your dog. Sorry! The party starts at three o'clock.
See you on Saturday,
Tara

c

Dear Linda,
Please come to my birthday party. Can you please bring your Purple Pumpkins CDs and your High Five CD? Please ask your brother to come, too. Jamie wants to play football with him. The party is at my grandma's house – 16 Station Road. It starts at four o'clock.
See you there!
Emma

2 Write an invitation to your party.

Remember to write: where it is.
                     what day it is.
                     what time it is.

Skills

1 Listen and colour.

Jolly

Poppy

2 Draw a clown face and play the game.

Has your clown got … hair?

Yes, he has.

Has your clown got … eyes?

No, she hasn't.

Listening and speaking

Learn and think: The life cycle of a butterfly

1 Listen, read and write the words.

1. The butterfly starts as a very small egg on a leaf. Butterfly eggs can be many shapes.

2. What comes from the egg? Not a butterfly, but a caterpillar! The caterpillar eats a lot of the leaves on the plants around it. It grows bigger and bigger.

3. When the caterpillar stops growing, it has a hard, brown skin called a chrysalis. The chrysalis hangs from a plant. Inside the chrysalis, the caterpillar is changing.

4. When the chrysalis opens, a butterfly comes out. After a few hours, the butterfly opens its wings and flies away.

> chrysalis   butterfly   egg   caterpillar

2 Read again and tick (✓) the boxes.

1. All caterpillar eggs are round.   yes ☐ / no ☐
2. The butterfly comes out of the egg.   yes ☐ / no ☐
3. Chrysalises are soft.   yes ☐ / no ☐
4. The butterfly comes out of the chrysalis.   yes ☐ / no ☐

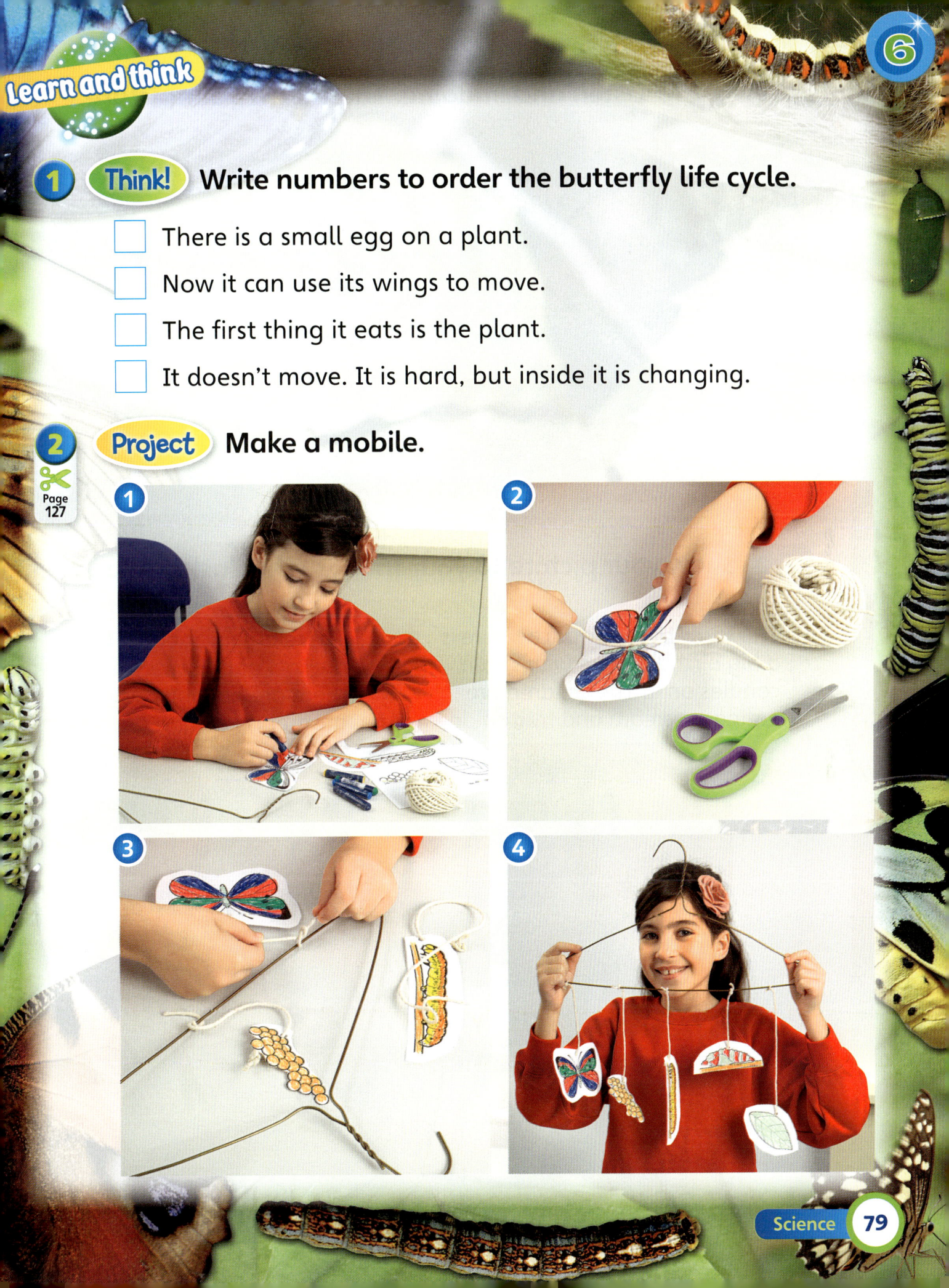

Learn and think

1 Think! Write numbers to order the butterfly life cycle.

☐ There is a small egg on a plant.

☐ Now it can use its wings to move.

☐ The first thing it eats is the plant.

☐ It doesn't move. It is hard, but inside it is changing.

2 Project Make a mobile.

Page 127

Science 79

Create that!

1 🎵 CD 3 · 17 Listen and imagine. Then draw your picture.

2 Show your picture to your friends. Then ask and answer.

This is my birthday party. Here is a big birthday cake with seven candles on it. The children are eating ice cream and fruit salad.

These are my friends. There are lots of presents and there are balloons. My brother is wearing a crown.

80 Creativity

Act out a birthday party

1 **Look, read and plan.**

At birthday parties people eat their favourite foods and give presents. They have lots of fun playing games and listening to music.

PARTY PLAN
- **Time:** 01:00 Saturday afternoon.
- **Place:** my house.
- **Food:** sandwiches, cake, ice cream, juice.
- **Games:** tug of war, three-legged race.

Useful language

Child 1
Happy Birthday!

Thanks, the … is very good.
Let's play … !

Child 2
Thanks!
Thank you for your present.
Have some …

Yes, good idea. /
No, I don't like …

2 **Act out your play.**

Happy Birthday!

Thanks! Have some cake.

Revision

7 Off we go!

1 Listen and look. Then listen and say the words.

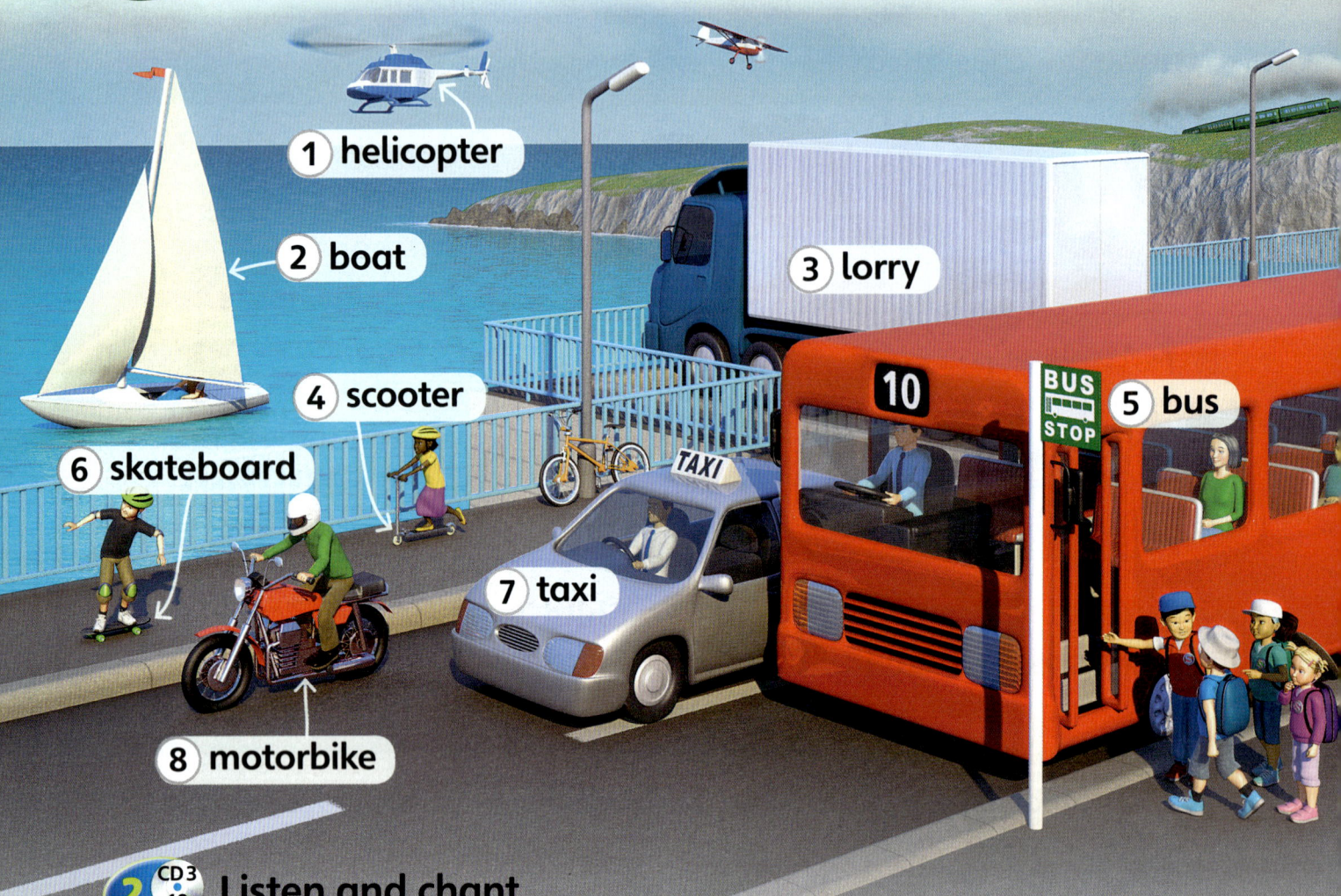

1. helicopter
2. boat
3. lorry
4. scooter
5. bus
6. skateboard
7. taxi
8. motorbike

2 Listen and chant.

Jump on a scooter.
Jump on a bus.
Jump on a motorbike,
And come with us!

Jump on a plane.
Jump on a boat.
Jump on a skateboard,
And off we go!

Jump in a helicopter.
Jump in a car.
Jump on a bike,
Are we going far?

Jump in a taxi.
Jump on a train.
Jump in a lorry,
Let's go again!

Transport

1 Match the children with the pictures. Then write the words.

1 **Paul** — I'd like to drive a _____.

2 **Mary** — I'd like to fly a _____.

3 **Eric** — I'd like to ride a _____.

4 **Ruth** — I'd like to sail a _____.

a helicopter
b boat
c train
d motorbike

2 **Grammar focus** Listen and say.

I'd like to go to Africa by plane.
I'd like to go to the jungle by train.

3 Talk about your dream holiday.

I'd like to go to the jungle by motorbike!

I'd like to …

1 **Listen and sing.**

It's a big, wide world out there,
And there's so much to see.
I'd like to fly around the world,
Why don't you come with me … ?

I'd like to go to Africa,
I'd like to see a snake.
I'd like to take it to my house,
And feed it bread and cake.
It's a big, wide …

I'd like to go to Canada,
I'd like to see a bear.
I'd like to take it to my house,
And give it boots to wear.
It's a big, wide …

I'd like to go to Italy,
I'd like to eat ice cream.
I'd like to take some to my house,
It isn't just a dream.
It's a big, wide …

2 **Think!** **Listen again and number the pictures.**

84 Singing for pleasure

1 Read and match.

1. What are you doing?
   I'm waiting for a bus.

2. What is John doing?
   He's playing with his cars.

3. What is Sally doing?
   She's sailing a boat.

4. What are you doing?
   I'm looking for my skateboard.

2 Grammar focus — Listen and say.

What **are you doing**?
Are you flying a plane?
I'm flying a plane.
Yes, I am. / No, I'm not.

3 Play the mime game.

What are you doing?
Are you … ?

Yes, I am. / No, I'm not. I'm …

Questions and answers with verb + *ing*   85

1 The bus trip

1
- A day at the beach!
- I'm excited.
- Off we go!

2
- The bus isn't moving.
- Why?
- Let's ask the driver.

3
- There are lots of sheep on the road. Look!
- No problem. I can help.

4
- We'd like to go to the beach.
- OK. Have a good day!

5
- Thanks.
- No problem.

6
- Oh no. We've got a problem with the tyre.
- I think I can help.

86 Value: being generous

7 Thanks.

You're welcome.

8 Here we are!
Where's the beach?
This is the bus to the airport.
Now it's my turn to help you! Let's go to the beach!

2 Look at the story and find the things. Write the numbers of the pictures.

☐ a plane ☐ a boat ☐ a motorbike
☐ a bike ☐ a helicopter ☐ a taxi

3 Find who says … *It's my turn to help y**ou**!*

4 CD 3 · 28 Listen and say.

L**uke**'s ch**ew**ing S**ue**'s n**ew** bl**ue** sh**oes**!

Phonics focus 87

Skills

1 Listen to your teacher and stick.

Museum of Transport

2 Look and say. The bird is …

88 Speaking

Skills

1 🎧 CD3 31 **Listen and number the pictures.**

2 **Read and tick (✓) the things that the car has got.**

This car is amazing because it's very long. Inside there are TVs and beds and a lot of sofas for all your friends. There is even a swimming pool!

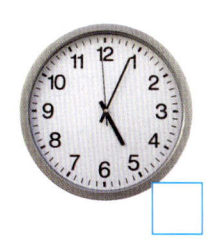

This car doesn't go on the roads very often. It is very difficult to drive. You need two drivers; one at the front and one at the back. They use this car in films or for special parties. Would you like to go for a drive in it?

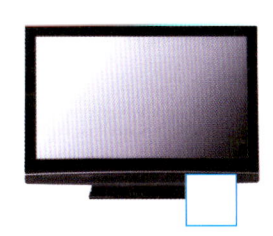

3 **Draw and write about an amazing car, bus, train or plane.**

This is my bus. It's blue and red. It's very big. It's got a bed in it. I'd like to go to China in it with my dad.

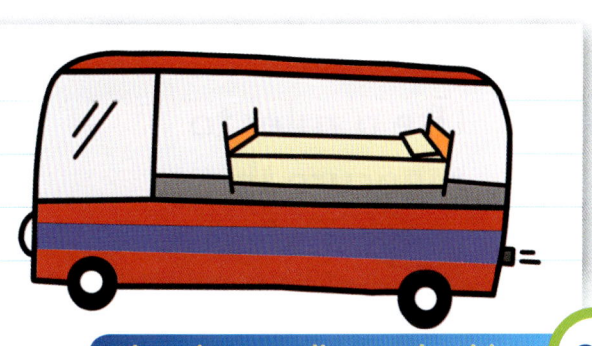

Listening, reading and writing

Measuring

1 Look and read. Write *a* or *b*.

We measure things to find out how big they are.

We can measure height and length.

height: line _____
length: line _____

2 Read, look and measure.

To measure small things we use centimetres (cm) and millimetres (mm). There are 10 millimetres in every centimetre. A ruler helps us to measure small things. Let's use it to measure the length of the pencils. Pencil A is 5cm long. Pencil B is 5cm and 7mm long. We write this as 5.7cm. Write the lengths for pencils C and D.

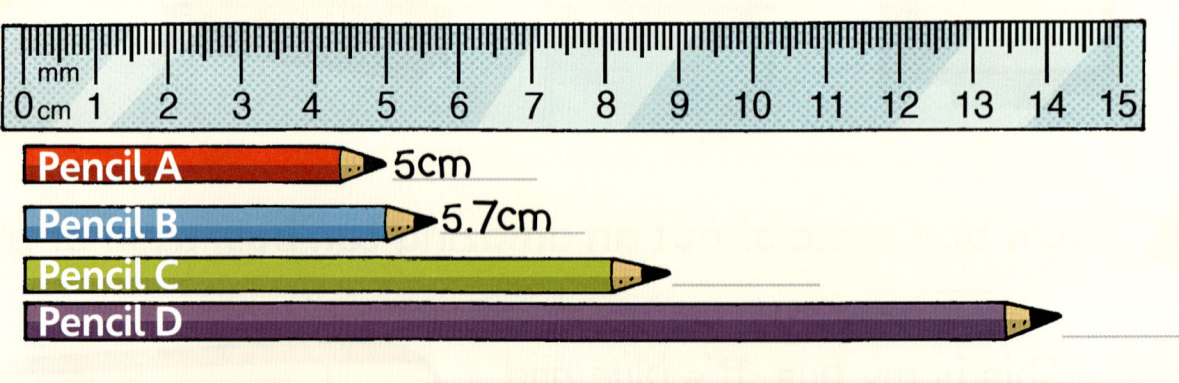

Pencil A — 5cm
Pencil B — 5.7cm
Pencil C — _____
Pencil D — _____

3 Use a ruler to measure things on your desk.

My rubber is 2.5cm long.

Learn and think

1 **Read, look and measure.**

To measure big things we use metres (m). There are 100 centimetres in one metre. A tape measure helps us to measure big things. Let's use it to measure the children's heights. Jane is 1m tall. Ollie is 1m and 25cm tall (1.25m). How tall are Nora and Jim?

Jane 1m   Ollie 1.25 m   Nora _____   Jim _____

2 Use a tape measure to measure the height of three friends.

3 *Project* *Think!* **Guess and measure.**

1. Draw a table and write five things that you want to measure.
2. Guess the length/height and write it in your *Guess* column.
3. Measure and write your results.

I want to measure	Guess	Measurement
The door (height)	2m	The door is 2.10m high.
My desk (length)	1.2m	My desk is 1.23m long.

Maths

Do that!

1 Listen and act out with your teacher.
Then listen again and number the pictures.

2 Read and number the sentences from the story.

- Look down! There's a puddle in front of you.
- The rain stops. Close your umbrella.
- You're waiting for bus number 11.
- Open your umbrella.
- Jump out of the way.
- It's starting to rain.
- Too late! Splash!
- Look, here comes a bus.

3 Listen to your friend and act out.

It's starting to rain.

92 Creativity

The roads and rail tracks game

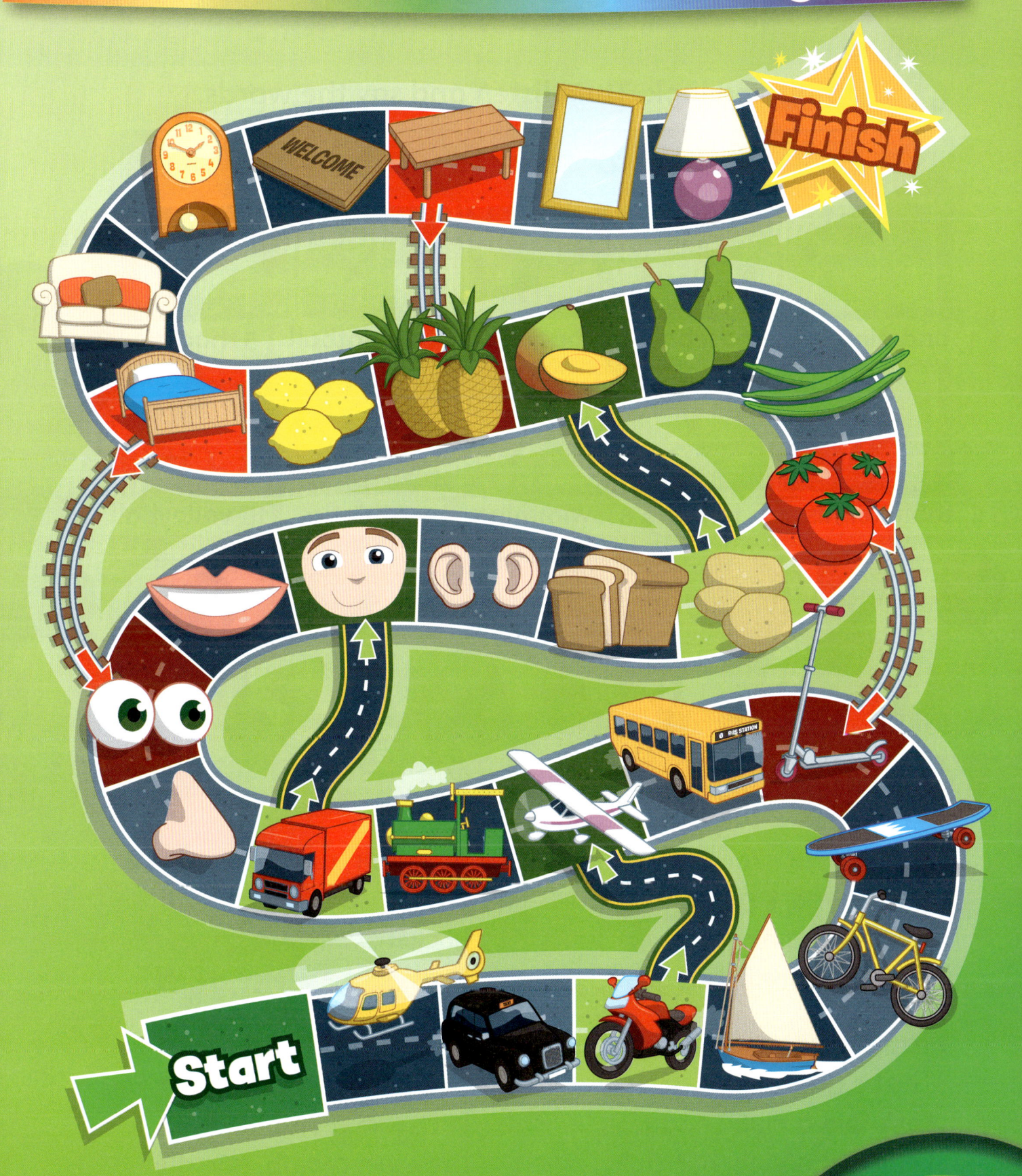

7

Revision 93

8 Sports club

1 Listen and look. Then listen and say the words.

Join a sports club

1 badminton 2 baseball 3 basketball 4 football 5 hockey
6 table tennis 7 tennis 8 swimming 9 athletics 10 volleyball

2 Listen and chant.

Football, basketball,
Lots of sport to do.
Tennis, badminton,
Let's do it – me and you.

Table tennis and athletics,
That's great fun – don't forget it.
Let's join a club today.
Let's join a club, hurray!

Baseball and swimming,
Lots of sport to do.
Hockey, volleyball,
Let's do it – me and you.

Table tennis and athletics,
That's great fun – don't forget it.
Let's join a club today.
Let's join a club, hurray!

1 Look and draw lines from the pictures to the sentences. Then listen and number the pictures.

a

Swimming is fun.

Playing tennis is difficult.

c

b

Dancing is great.

d

Playing baseball is boring.

2 **Grammar focus** Listen and say.

Flying a kite's difficult.   **Riding**'s great.

3 Look and draw lines. Then ask and answer.

flying   watching   listening to   reading

painting   making   riding   playing

What do you think about flying a kite?

Flying a kite's …

ing forms   95

1 **Listen and sing.**

Playing tennis is great fun.
It's fun for everyone.
So come on, everyone,
Come and join the fun!

Flying kites is easy,
Easy for you and me.
So come and fly with me,
Oh, come on, it's so easy!
It's so easy!

Singing songs is great fun.
It's fun for everyone.
So come on, everyone,
Come and join the fun!

Painting pictures is easy.
Easy for you and me.
So come and paint with me,
Oh, come on, it's so easy!
It's so easy!
Come and join the fun.

2 **Choose words and read out your new verse.**

Playing music is great fun.
It's fun for everyone ...

Singing for pleasure

1 Listen and number the pictures.

2 Grammar focus — Listen and say.

What sport do you **like doing**?
I **like** swimming.   So do I. / Me too.
I **like playing** football.   I don't.

3 Ask and answer.

What sport do you like doing?

I like …

Like + ing 97

1 The football club

1. Can I join the football team? — Sorry, the team's full.

2. You can join the table tennis club. — Table tennis is boring. I like playing football.

3. I know! Let's start a football team. — OK.

4. Join our team!

5. Do you want to play a game? — Ha, ha. It's going to be very easy.

6. Goal! — Well done, Flash!

98 Value: including people

7 Great goal, Misty!

Come on. Try harder, Green team.

8 Do you want to be in my team?

Yellow team 2 — Green team 0

No, thank you. We've got our team.

2 **Read and tick (✓) the boxes.**

1 The boys' football team is full. yes ☐ / no ☐
2 Flash wants to play tennis. yes ☐ / no ☐
3 Flash and Misty start a team. yes ☐ / no ☐
4 The boy thinks his team is going to win. yes ☐ / no ☐
5 Thunder scores a goal. yes ☐ / no ☐

3 **Find who says …** Great goal, Misty!

4 **Listen and say.** CD 3 43

A hipp**o** and a g**oa**t with a h**o**le in their b**oa**t.

Phonics focus 99

Skills

1 Listen and tick (✓) the boxes.

	football		tennis		swimming		basketball		volleyball		athletics	
	☺	☹	☺	☹	☺	☹	☺	☹	☺	☹	☺	☹
Jenny												
Ian												

2 Ask and answer.

What's your favourite sport?

swimming |||| |||
football |||| ||

It's …

3 Now write about your class and make a bar chart.

OUR FAVOURITE SPORTS

In our class there are 22 children.
8 children's favourite sport is swimming.
7 children's favourite sport is football.
3 children's favourite sport is athletics.
2 children's favourite sport is table tennis.
2 children's favourite sport is tennis.

Listening, speaking and writing

Skills

1 Look and read. Write *yes* or *no*.

1. The children are in the park.
2. There are 14 children.
3. The girls are playing hockey.
4. The girls are wearing yellow T-shirts.
5. The boys are playing baseball.
6. The boy's ball is orange.

Breathing

1 🎧 CD3 47 **Listen and read about sport and breathing. Write the words.**

When you do sport, you often breathe a lot. When you breathe, the air moves in and out of the lungs. Put your hands on your chest and see what happens when you breathe in and breathe out.

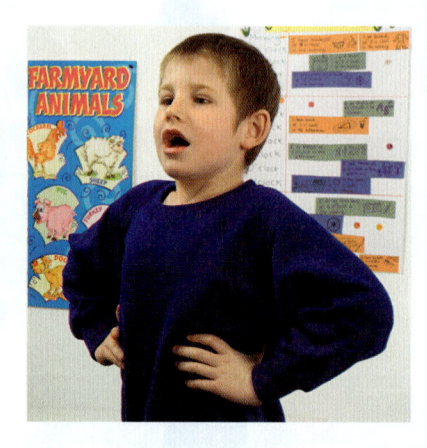

> breathing in   breathing out

2 *Think!* **Find out how much breath there is in your lungs.**

1. Write down how tall you are.
2. Take a balloon and take a deep breath.
3. Now blow all the air in your lungs into the balloon.
4. Ask a friend to tie a string around the mouth of the balloon.
5. Now measure around your balloon and write your result. Look at your friends' results. What do you notice?

Learn and think

1 **Project** Find out more about breathing and sport.

When you do sport, you breathe a lot because your lungs need more air.

1. Count how many times you breathe in one minute. Write the number.
2. Run on the spot for one minute.
3. Now count how many times you breathe for one minute after running. Write the number.
4. Now time your friend.

2 Now make a bar code for your class.

Science 103

Create that!

1 🎧 CD3 48 Listen and imagine. Then draw your picture.

2 Write about your picture. Then listen to your friends and guess.

My trophy is yellow. It's very big and very beautiful. It's a trophy for tennis.

Sports graffiti poster

1 **Think!** Make a poster.

a Choose a sport and find pictures.

b Stick the pictures on a big, colourful piece of paper.

c Do you like the sport? Is it easy or difficult? Write on your poster.

2 Talk about sport.   I like playing football …

Revision 105

9 Holiday plans

1 Listen and look. Then listen and say the words.

1. visit my cousins
2. go hiking
3. keep a scrapbook
4. help in the garden
5. build a tree house
6. read a comic
7. learn to swim
8. go camping
9. take riding lessons

2 Listen and chant.

Give me a **G**!
Go camping.
Give me an **H**!
Help in the garden.
Give me a **V**!
Visit my cousins.
Give me a **K**!
Keep a scrapbook.

Give me an **L**!
Learn how to swim.
Give me a **B**!
Build a tree house.
Give me a **G**!
Go hiking.
Give me an **H**!
Holiday! **H**oliday! **H**oliday!

106 Holidays

1 Look, read and write the names. Then listen and check.

Emma   Ben   Kate   Tom

1 Can we visit Grandpa tomorrow afternoon?

2 Can I build a tree house tomorrow afternoon?

3 Can I go horse riding tomorrow morning?

4 Can we have pizza at *Ruby's* tomorrow evening?

2 Grammar focus   Listen and say.

> Can I go horse riding tomorrow morning?
> Can we visit Grandpa and Grandma in the afternoon?

3 Ask and answer.

What would you like to do in the holidays?

Can I … ?

Can for requests   107

1 **Listen and sing.**

It's time for a holiday,
A holiday, a holiday,
It's time for a holiday,
Hurray, hurray, hurray …

Can I build a tree house,
In my grandma's apple tree?
I'm going to sleep and play there,
Come on, please join me!

It's time for a holiday …

Can I go camping,
On a sandy beach, oh yeah?
Can I go swimming?
Why don't you join me there?

It's time for a holiday …

Can I take riding lessons,
With Michael, James and Lynn?
They're my favourite cousins,
Come on, please join in!

It's time for a holiday …

2 **Listen again and tick (✓) the things that you hear in the song.**

1. 2. 3. 4. 5. 6.

Singing for pleasure

1 Think! Read and match. Then listen and check.

1. Does your sister eat tomatoes?
2. How old is your brother?
3. Can you swim?
4. Have spiders got six legs?
5. What's her name?
6. What's his name?
7. What does your sister like to eat?
8. Where are my pencils?
9. Would you like an orange?
10. Is there any milk in the house?
11. When's her birthday?
12. Whose jumper is pink?

a. No, there isn't any.
b. It's Oliver.
c. It's Kate.
d. Emily's.
e. In November.
f. Yes, I can.
g. Yes, please.
h. No, she doesn't.
i. He's thirteen.
j. Under the desk.
k. Chicken with rice.
l. No, they've got eight.

2 Play the question game.

Would you like an orange? — Yes, please.

Revision

Dream holidays

1
- It looks great.
- Can we come up?
- I'd like to build a tree house.

2
- I like swimming.
- Me too!
- And what would you like to do, Whisper?
- I'd like to learn to swim.

3
- Where are you, Misty?
- We can't find you.
- I'm behind you!
- What would you like to do, Misty?
- I'd like to visit my cousins.

4
- Can you get me the tomatoes, please?
- Here you are, Grandma.
- What about you, Flash?
- I'd like to help my grandma in the garden.

110 Value: helping people

5 Come with me, kids.

6 Happy holiday! Thank you very much. Hurray!

2 Read and write who says …

1 I'd like to help my grandma …
2 I'd like to learn to swim.
3 I'd like to build a tree house.
4 I'm behind you!

3 Find who says … I'd like to visit my cousins.

4 Listen and say.

The **z**oo keeper give**s** the li**z**ard**s** banana**s** for dinner.

Phonics focus 111

Skills

1 Look and read. Put a tick (✓) or a cross (✗) in the box.

1 This is a hippo. ☐

2 This is a swimming pool. ☐

3 These are some grapes. ☐

4 This is a ball. ☐

5 This is a scrapbook. ☐

6 This is a lorry. ☐

Skills

1 **Listen and stick.**

2 **Look, think and answer the questions.**

There are ... in the picture.

1 How many children are in the picture?
2 What is the boy in the black T-shirt doing?
3 What is the man wearing?
4 There is a boy next to the river. What colour is his cap?
5 What are the boys in red T-shirts doing?

Listening and speaking

Learn and think

Fairy tales

1 Read and tick (✓).

What do you read on holiday?

☐ magazines ☐ comics ☐ story books

2 Listen, read and answer the questions.

The Flower Queen's Daughter

Characters: Dragon, Mother Dragon, Flower Queen, Flower Queen's Daughter, King of the Foxes, Prince

Fairy tales like *The Flower Queen's Daughter* are stories for children. They are often about characters like kings, queens, dragons, witches and animals that can talk. Two famous fairy tale writers were the Brothers Grimm from Germany. Some of their stories are *Rumpelstiltskin*, *Snow White*, *Sleeping Beauty*, *Rapunzel*, *Cinderella*, and *Hansel and Gretel*.

The American film studio Walt Disney makes films of famous fairy tales. Some of these are *Aladdin*, *The Little Mermaid* and *Pinocchio*.

a Which fairy tales do you know?
b What are they called in your country?
c Why do you think people like fairy tales?

The Brothers Grimm

114 Literature

Learn and think

1 Think! Read and match.

Fairy tales are often about good and bad characters. Here are the good characters from three fairy tales. Match them with the bad characters from the same fairy tales.

1 The three Billy Goats Gruff want to cross the bridge.

a The ugly sisters make her clean the house.

2 Cinderella wants to go to a party at the palace.

b The wicked witch can give her some legs.

3 The little mermaid wants to leave the sea and live on the land.

c There is a troll under the bridge. He is very hungry.

2 Project Choose your favourite fairy tale and act it out.

Literature 115

Do that!

1 🎧 CD3 64 **Listen and act out with your teacher. Then listen again and number the pictures.**

2 Read and number the sentences from the story.

- ☐ The cow runs away.
- ☐ You wake up.
- ☐ Open the tent.
- ☐ Clap your hands and shout, 'Boo!'
- ☐ You are sleeping in your tent.
- ☐ There's a cow outside.
- ☐ Stand up and say, 'I'm a Super Friend!'
- ☐ Listen.

3 Listen to your friend and act out.

Open the tent.

116 Creativity

Quiz time

1. Would you like to go … in the holidays?
   a camp   b camping   c tent

2. … go swimming?
   a Can I   b Would I   c Who

3. What are they doing?
   a hiking   b helping Grandma
   c building a tree house

4. What … your mum like for breakfast?
   a is   b do   c does

5. Thunder would like to …
   a learn to swim.
   b learn to ride a horse.
   c build a tree house.

6. Flash would like to …
   a learn to swim.   b help her grandma.
   c visit her cousins.

7. Circle the different sound.
   a give**s**   b **bus**   c **z**oo

8. The Brothers Grimm were from …
   a England.   b Mexico.   c Germany.

Revision

Festivals and cut-outs

Halloween

Cut-outs 119

Cut-outs

Christmas

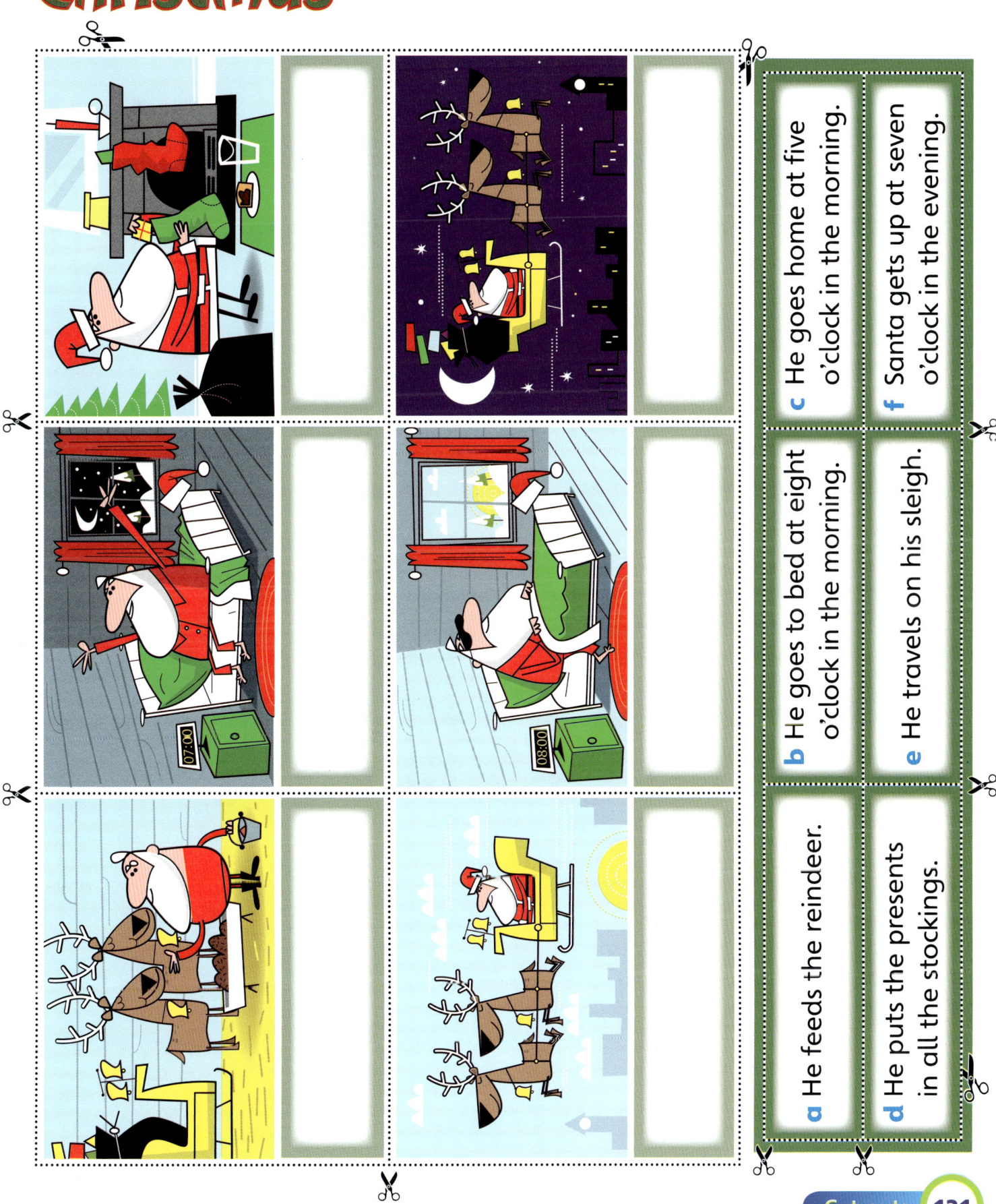

- **a** He feeds the reindeer.
- **b** He goes to bed at eight o'clock in the morning.
- **c** He goes home at five o'clock in the morning.
- **d** He puts the presents in all the stockings.
- **e** He travels on his sleigh.
- **f** Santa gets up at seven o'clock in the evening.

Cut-outs 121

EASTER

Cut-outs 123

124 Cut-outs

Unit 3 Cut-out (page 37)

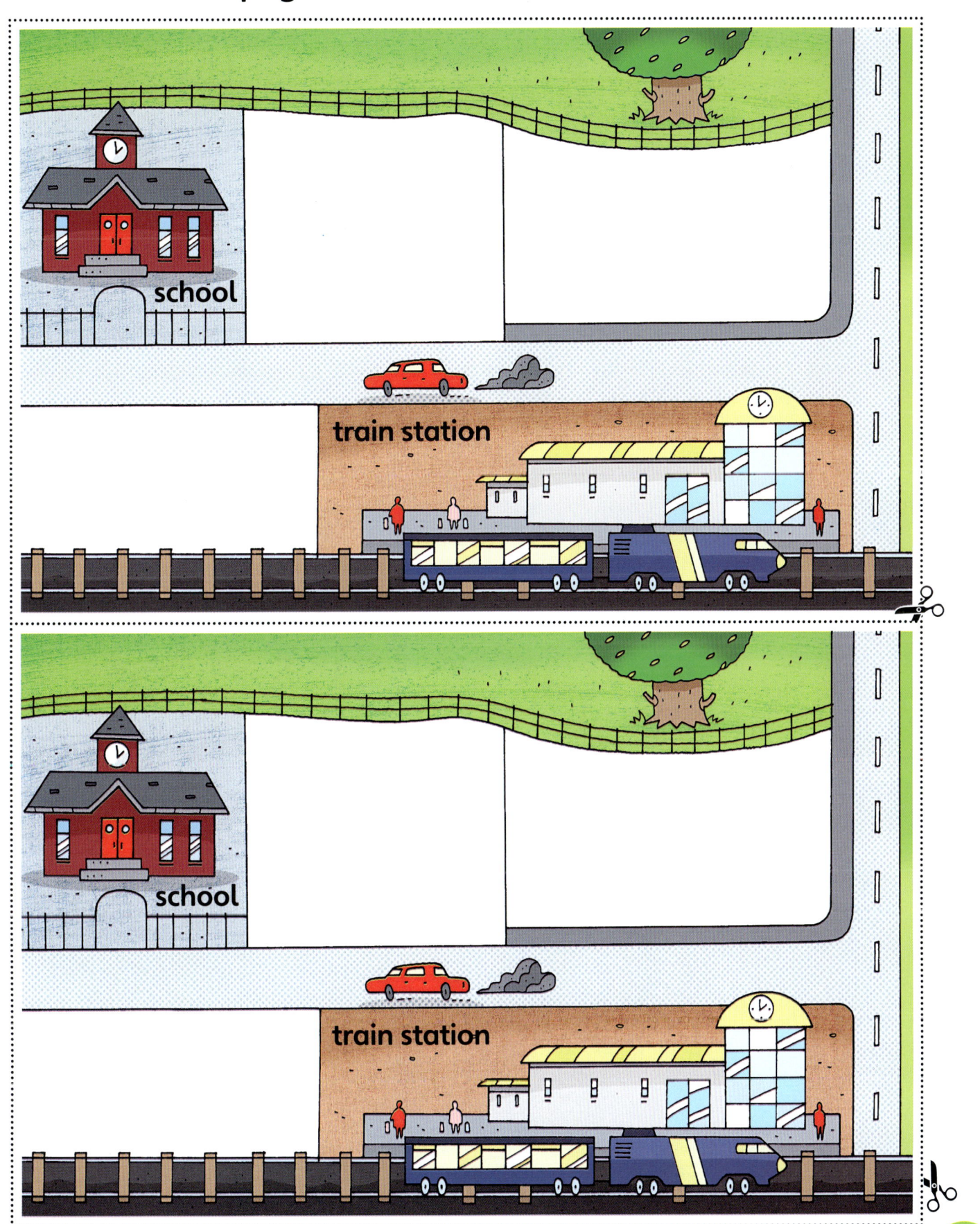

school

train station

school

train station

Cut-outs 125

Unit 6 Cut-out (page 79)

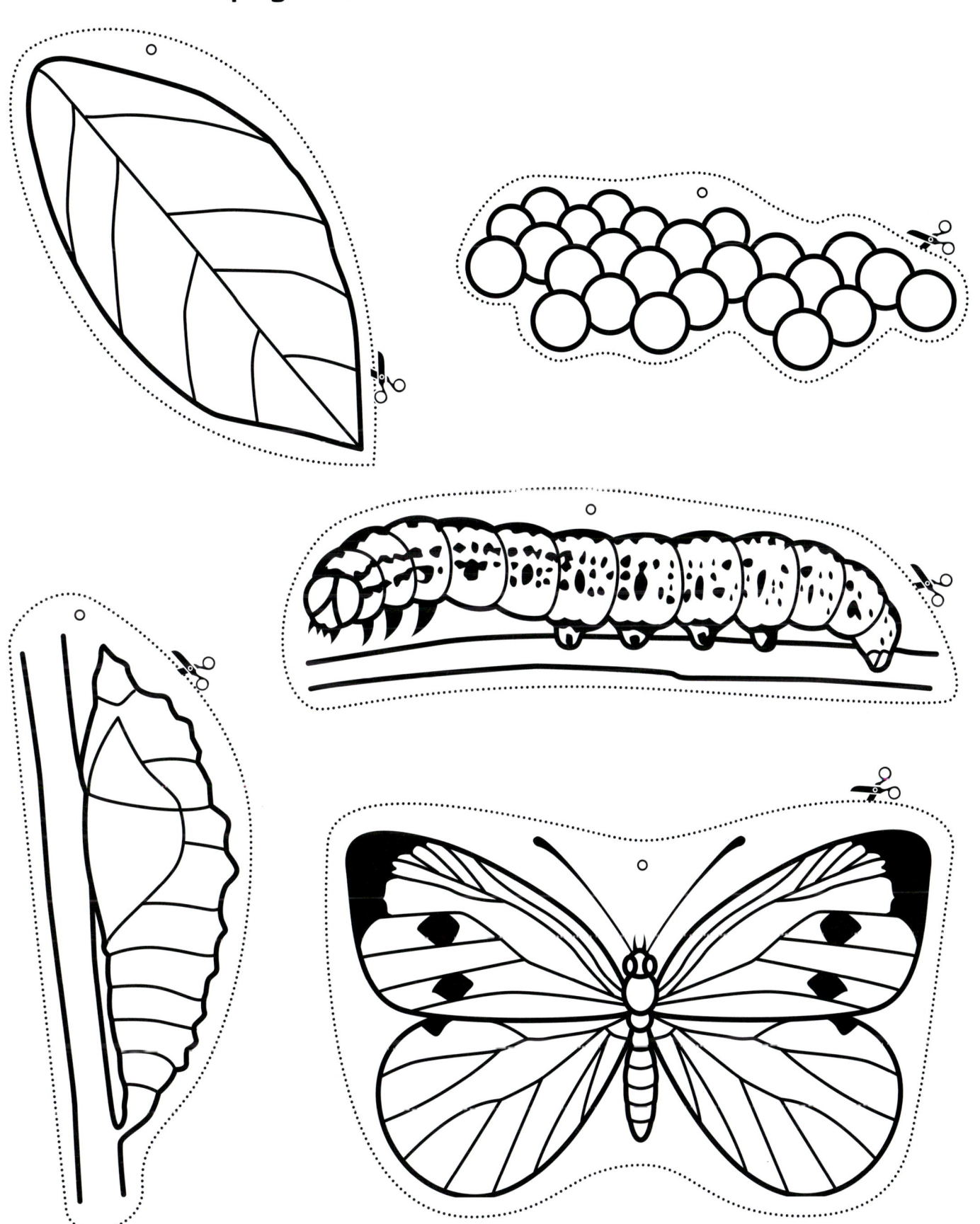

Cut-outs 127

128 Cut-outs